An Illustrated Guide
to the Medieval Wall Paintings
in the Church of Saint Mary the Virgin
at Chalgrove in the County of Oxfordshire

Robert W Heath-Whyte

The Parochial Church Council of St. Mary's Church, Chalgrove

Fig 1. The north wall.

Fig 2. The south wall.

For Carole, Edward, David and Joanna

Published by the Parochial Church Council of St.Mary's Church, 132 High Street, Chalgrove, Oxfordshire, OX44 7ST,UK.

May 2003

ISBN 0-9544681-0-4

Printed by Lynx DPM Limited, 35A Monument Business Park, Chalgrove, Oxfordshire, OX44 7RW

The proceeds of sales of this book go to the Restoration Fund of St.Mary's Church, Chalgrove.

Front cover Saint Mary holding the Christ child from the Jesse Tree painting on the north wall of the church.

Back cover St.Mary's Church, Chalgrove, in winter.
Background pattern of six-leaved fleur-de-lys as scattered around the wall paintings.

Fig.3 Monumental brasses to the De Barentyn family in the chancel floor

CONTENTS

INTRODUCTION

The chancel of Chalgrove church is one of the most complete works of art of the first half of the fourteenth century in England. Clearly it was built and decorated in one sustained campaign. What is more, due to the deciphering of the inscriptions above the lowest paintings on the east wall, we have the names of some at least of the donors – 'dominorum Wabor...', the Lords of Warborough, the Barentin family, who shared the Lordship of Chalgrove with the de Plessis family, whose manor house survives. The inscription referring to the Barentins is in close proximity to the picture of the Harrowing of Hell, so it could well be a plea for the souls of departed members of the family. It is placed towards the conclusion of the scenes along the north side of the life and passion of Christ. Opposite it, on the south side of the church, where the life of the Virgin is recounted, the prayer is addressed to her, and perhaps places the de Plessis family under her protection. Sir Drew Barentin was enlarging his manor between 1300 and 1320, so he was prosperous. It is also the case that in 1317 Edward II gave the church to Thame Abbey, with the special duty to pray for the soul of his favourite, murdered five years before. This donation is the most likely trigger for the rebuilding of the Chancel. It is quite possible that the building works were scarcely complete when Edward was murdered at Berkeley in 1327. The decoration of the chancel could then have passed to the local families. The choice of subject matter reflects the emphasis of their time. The Life of Christ is represented by its beginning and its end. There are no scenes of preaching or miracles. The Virgin has featured, of course, in the first scenes of the Incarnation.

The south wall picks up her story after Christ's Ascension, and is entirely Apochryphal. The Apostles visiting her empty tomb, and a rerun of the doubting Thomas theme, parallel elements in the Biblical Resurrection narratives. This choice of emphasis would be codified within two generations of the paintings at Chalgrove in the selection of the fifteen 'Mysteries' of the Rosary, an arrangement of devotional prayer under the headings of the five Joyful, five Sorrowful, and five Glorious themes of the Virgin's life. This devotional exercise was particularly fostered by the Dominicans, who had been active for a century in mission to the laity. It provided a framework for prayer suited to all occasions, it could easily be memorised, even by the unlettered.

There is only one point where I would disagree with the author of this remarkable guide book: he thinks that looking at wall paintings can be 'boring'. The nub of the matter is in their condition, but the trick is in seeing them as scattered pieces of a jig saw puzzle of which we have lost the picture on the lid. Show us a big toe and a fish, and we deduce St. Christopher, towering to the rafters. The corner of a lily in a vase speak of an Annunciation, the tail of a dragon and we can assume St. George. But we can only make these good guesses because we add together in our mind's eye many comparable examples. Here, for the first time, is a guide book where these close comparisons are brought together, and we can see how the pieces of the puzzle make sense. If all guide books to churches with wall paintings could be similarly illustrated, how wonderful that would be! Mr Heath-Whyte is also fortunate in being able to use sketches made of the paintings when they first came to light in the 1850's. At the height of the Gothic Revival, the early fourteenth century was thought by some architects to represent the apogee of Medieval Art, so he studied these images in respectful detail. His record sometimes tells us of figures or gestures now lost. He caught the notes, you might say, but he was not a good artist, and he missed the music. If you compare his prim version of the Virgin's mantle in the Jesse Tree (fig.10) or the Annunciation (fig.13) with the swinging grace of the originals (figs.11 and 14) you have the measure of what he could not convey. It is that leaping line, of ogee arch or swaying figure, that is the essence of what has been called Decorated art, and the essence of Chalgrove.

As Mr Heath-Whyte has observed, the painter would use the very irregularities of his space to suggest a couch to lean back on (fig.37) or Calvary to climb (fig.48). Many details of Medieval iconography are disarming in their simplicity. Christ ascends to Heaven, so we have only his feet and the bottom of his robe disappearing into a cloud (fig.67). St. Thomas holds out in delight the girdle the Virgin has dropped down for him as she soared to heaven, and proudly displays it to the other Apostles. The line of Christ's dead arm continues, with real pathos, into the line of the weeping Virgin as she kisses his hand. We are reminded of what Pietro Lorrenzetti made of the same motive at about the same time in the Lower Church of San Francesco in Assisi. The tomb of Christ with three recesses containing as many sleeping soldiers was carved at the same date to form an Easter Sepulchre in Lincoln Cathedral. It is possible a figure of the Risen Christ was once painted on the back wall at Lincoln, but at Chalgrove we have him leaping like Nijinski, with none of the sobriety Piero della Francesca brought to the subject one hundred years later.

Mr Heath-Whyte has devoted many years to deciphering the paintings at Chalgrove, their historical background, and a library of apposite comparisons. He has been supported by Mr Stephen Maynard who has generously put at his disposal and ours his MA Thesis written for the Centre for Medieval Studies at York University. This is the source for the debatable identification of the Judge as Annas rather than Pilate, (pp. 30-31) and for the renaming of the Entombment subject as the Anointing (pp. 42-43). It is not usual to have a separate scene for the anointing, and the entombment is an essential element in the cycle, so I would prefer the traditional name.

The people of Chalgrove, and the fund raising bodies who have helped them, have lavished their strength upon this church. May they now enjoy their labours in peace. But, if anything more has to be done in the future, I would be sorely tempted to explore behind one at least of the wall monuments that cover areas of the painting. Where they were fixed, the paintings will of course have gone, but there might be portions in the centre where the surface survives, and does so with freshness.

If there were a prize for the best guide book of a wall painted church, Chalgrove would be a front line contender. It will enhance the enjoyment of every visitor to the church, and remain an essential work of reference.

These paintings do not deal with quaint fables, but with the central story of the suffering, love, and the hope of mankind. The chancel of Chalgrove is an early fourteenth century prayer, articulated in a way even the illiterate villagers of the time would have understood, and which, with Mr Heath-Whyte's help, we can still understand.

Dr. Tudor-Craig, F.S.A. (Pamela Lady Wedgwood)

Sometime Chairman of the Wall Paintings Committee of the Council for the Care of Churches.
27 January 2003

AUTHOR'S ACKNOWLEDGEMENTS

I acknowledgement gratefully the help which I have received from many people in the research and preparation of this book over the past few months and years.

In particular I thank the sponsors of this book, without whose generosity it would never have been printed, including The Idlewild Trust, Chalgrove Local History Group, St.Mary's Church Chalgrove PCC, "Murder at The Manor", Mary Crouch, Lady Pamela Mills and Barbara Slater. Thank you to Steven Maynard for generously giving me a copy of his Master's thesis and allowing me to use his findings without restraint; to Pamela Lady Wedgwood for her Introduction, her encouragement and her critique of the final draft; to Judith Bennett for her painstaking proof reading; to Bas Tindall for patiently holding the ladder while I took the final photos; to my fellow 'wall paintings guide' Jill Floyd for her encouragement and insights; and to the Vicars of St.Mary's, Rev'd Ian Cohen and his predecessor Rev'd Stephen Bartlett for their help and patience.

Copyright owners of the pictures which I have used to illuminate the wall paintings have been generous in agreeing to my use of these images and this is really appreciated as the pictures help to give an idea of the wealth of medieval art which there is still to be seen across Europe. A full listing of these pictures is on page 95.

The staff at all the Museums and Libraries which I have visited and contacted have been unfailingly polite and helpful despite the fact that they get hundreds of such enquiries from enthusiastic amateurs like me. I thank them all for their help.

Experts in their own fields of medieval study have also been generous with their time and knowledge; the late Eve Baker on wall paintings; Paul Binski on art and painters; Michelle Brown on interpreting the inscriptions; Jane Geddes on door hinges; John Blair on the moated manor in Harding's Field; William Leaf on the Bereford family; Rachel and Paul Jacques on the de Plessis family.

Friends, fellow Licensed Lay Ministers, colleagues at work, and visitors to the church have all added to the work-in-progress.

My family, especially my wife Carole and my children (now adult), have supported me all along the way, and to them I gratefully dedicate this book.

Bob Heath-Whyte
Chalgrove
30 March 2003

THE SETTING

"Not more boring old wall paintings!" Looking at old wall paintings in churches and museums can be boring, especially when the paintings are badly eroded or only partially visible, or when their content is obscure. The aim of this guide book is to make the wall paintings of Saint Mary's church, Chalgrove, interesting and understandable, by putting them in their context and alongside other examples of the same pictures in contemporary medieval art.

When and Who?

The Chancel of the church was completely renovated and redecorated sometime during the first half of the fourteenth century.

Edward II had come to the throne in 1307 but was not the sort of man who could successfully follow in the footsteps of Edward I. Robert the Bruce inflicted a humiliating defeat on him at the Battle of Bannockburn in 1314. The next few years were marked by floods, ruined harvests, and a resulting period of serious famine in which, in 1316, even the King had difficulty in buying bread for his household. Then in 1323, his wife Queen Isabella fled to France with her lover Roger Mortimer, returning eventually in September 1326 with the young Prince Edward (later Edward III) and an army which chased the King across the country, finally capturing him and deposing him, leaving him to a grim death in Berkeley Castle in September 1327. Queen Isabella had passed through Oxford during this campaign - is it possible that the Manors at Chalgrove provided both food and soldiers to support her army?

At this time Chalgrove had two overlords. The village was divided almost equally between the Barentin family, who resided in the Manor House which lay in what is now the field behind the Hardings, and the de Plessis family, whose once moated Manor House still stands in Mill Lane.

Between 1300 and 1320 Sir Drew Barentin II had a third phase of building carried out at his manor. Partly coincident with the work on the manor, during approximately 1310 to 1330, the chancel of the church of Saint Mary the Virgin, just a stone's throw from the manor, was completely rebuilt and redecorated. Who paid for this work to be done? There are two possible contenders. One is Sir Drew himself, perhaps jointly with the young Sir Edmund de Beresford, heir to the de Plessis manor. For the next five generations of the Barentin family this chancel became the family mausoleum, and across the painting of the Harrowing of Hell we find an

Fig 4. The memorial to Piers Gaveston at Leek Wooton.

inscription which appears to be a prayer for the souls of the Lords of Warborough, meaning the Barentins. The second contender is possibly King Edward II himself, though indirectly through the Abbey of Thame. King Edward gave the living of Chalgrove to Thame Abbey in 1317 so that the monks of Thame would say masses for the soul of Piers

Gaveston, his favourite who was murdered by the jealous barons on 1st July 1312 in a wood near Leek Wooton in Northamptonshire, Fig 4.

By tradition the chancel was the responsibility of the patron, in this case Thame Abbey or the Abbot of Thame, and certainly any works carried out in the chancel after 1317 would have required the approval of the Abbot.

Fig 5. The sedilia in the south wall of the Chancel.

The complete scheme of redecoration would have included the construction of the sedilia (seats) and lavabo (wash basin) in the south wall of the chancel, Fig 5, stained glass in all the windows, and it is possible that it also included a new rood screen across the chancel entrance. Even the hinges on the door in the south wall of the chancel were new, Fig 6. The distinctive flat terminals of the "foliage" of these hinges with the full curves on the leaves date from 1350 to 1400 AD so either the hinges were not completed until after the renovation scheme or we have to date the complete renovation to some time after 1350.

Then two hundred years later came the Reformation in England. In 1535 the Bishops of the Church of England officially selected the "Zurich" numbering of the Ten Commandments which made the second commandment "Thou shalt not make for thyself any graven image". As Diarmaid MacCulloch states in his book "Thomas Cranmer", "England was now falteringly set on the path to the destruction of images, which would be one of the most marked features of its Reformation."

One of the Injunctions issued by King Edward VI in 1547 decreed that "Also, That they shall take away, utterly extinct and destroy all shrines, covering of shrines, all tables, candlesticks, trindilles or rolls of War, pictures, paintings, and all other monuments of feigned miracles, pilgrimages, Idolatory and Superstition : so that there remain no memory of the

Fig 6. The 14th century hinges on the inside of the door in the south wall of the Chancel.

same in walls, glass windows, or elsewhere within their Churches or Houses..." and so our wall paintings were covered over with limewash and they were indeed forgotten. If the stained glass windows were not destroyed at the same time then they would certainly have been destroyed subsequently by Cromwell's Protestants during the Civil War.

Time passed and along came the Victorians and their enthusiasm for church "restoration", and for antiquities. In the year 1858, during a course of restoration work which he was carrying out, the Reverend Robert French Lawrence re-discovered the medieval wall paintings in the chancel. Being an enlightened and educated man, he recognised them for the work of art which they are and brought them to the attention of the antiquarians, and made sure that they were completely uncovered and recorded by artists, the first of whom were his own daughters.

During the next one hundred years, various techniques were developed for better preservation of wallpaintings, whether Ancient Egyptian, Roman or Medieval English, and in 1975, 1978, 1986 and 1993 these techniques were used on respectively the south, east and north walls of the chancel at Chalgrove. Unfortunately, erosion caused by damp has lost some of the detail and colour of the paintings on the north wall, while the placing of two large monuments in the south wall before the re-discovery of the paintings has destroyed two complete scenes. However, we now have one of the most complete sets of medieval church wall paintings here in our chancel.

How?

It would be interesting if we knew something about the person who painted these murals, but their identity is lost to us while their skill remains to delight us still. Professor E W Tristram in 1933 stated that "the work belongs to the East Anglian school" and dated the paintings to be "executed in the second quarter of the 14th century".

The subjects and the formality of the positions and gestures of the characters in each picture are part of the rich symbolism of Christian art of this period and are discussed for each picture.

The painter would have started by dividing the wall space up with boundary lines for each picture. Such lines are still visible in some schemes in other churches but have disappeared here. Next the artist would have sketched out each scene using charcoal. It is quite likely that he would have used templates for recurring items such as the head of Mary as there is striking similarity between its execution in several places, remembering that such a template could be used to produce reverse facing images too. See Fig 8 for the stencil or template used to draw the flowers. After sketching, the artist then would have gone over the main outlines with red ochre. Then using the basic earth colours of red ochre, yellow ochre, lamp black, and white the artist would have used his eye and skill to fill in the flesh and hair colours, the drapery and drops of gore, the vitality and simple beauty that we can still see today.

What and why?

A 13th century Bishop wrote "Pictures and ornaments in churches are the lessons and scriptures of the laity… for what writing supplies to him who can read, that does a picture supply to him who is unlearned and can only look." But that statement belies the complexity of symbolism to be found within medieval pictures which requires the viewer to have a certain amount of knowledge in order to be able to interpret them.

There are two main aspects to this symbolism, or iconography. One is the way in which the Saints point to their symbols so as to tell us who they are, for example, Saint Paul points to his sword and Saint John the Baptist points to the Lamb of God. Secondly colour is used as a "code". Unfortunately all the colours in our paintings have faded so what was once

a dark blue on Mary's dresses is now black, but blue is Mary's colour and she wears it throughout our paintings until her death - more of that later. Yellow is the colour of treachery and

Fig 7. Mary's flower symbol

identifies Judas for us in a nearly obliterated scene. So the symbols and colours tell us a lot about the stories in each picture.

Apart from her colour code, Mary also has her own symbol of a flower. This is variously described as the lily, tulip, iris or fleur de lys and in one piece of medieval writing, the Ayenbite of Inwyt dated 1340, this symbol is described as having six leaves or petals which represent the six attributes of Mary's maidenhood as follows, "holiness and purity of body, purity of heart, meekness, fear of God, austerity of life and steadfastness." What a role model ! The chancel of our church is of course covered in Mary's symbol, the pink six petaled flowers which are scattered above and between the other paintings. These would have been painted using a leaden stencil

such as the one pictured which was found at Meaux Abbey in Yorkshire. This stencil produced flowers which were 70mm in diameter, the same size as the flowers on our walls.

Fig 8. Lead stencil from Meaux Abbey, Yorkshire.

So for the medieval viewers the wall paintings were visual reminders of well known stories and biblical truths and were an integral part of their worship and prayer. Lady Wedgwood mentions in her Introduction the five Joyful, five Sorrowful and five Glorious mysteries of Mary as used in reciting prayer with a rosary. Of the five Joyful mysteries we have three in the wall paintings, the Annunciation, the Nativity and the Presentation in the Temple - the other two are the Visit of Mary to Elizabeth and the Finding of the boy Jesus in the Temple. Of the five Sorrowful mysteries we have four, the Crowning with Thorns, the Scourging at the Pillar, the Carrying of the Cross and the Crucifixion, only the Agony in the Garden is missing. Of the five Glorious mysteries we have four, the Resurrection, the Ascension, the Assumption of the Blessed Virgin Mary, and the Crowning of Mary as Queen of Heaven, the fifth one being the Descent of the Holy Spirit on the Apostles. Formal worship in a medieval church centred on the Mass and the average citizen of Chalgrove would probably have received communion once a year at Easter. For the rest of the year the highlight at each Mass was the elevation of the Host by the priest after the sacring, the prayer in which the transubstantiation was believed to take place. Just before the sacring a bell was rung so that each member of the "congregation" could leave whatever private devotions they were making and make sure that they could see the elevated host. Just to see it was sufficient and could produce claims of miraculous results. For the rest of the service individuals could make their own prayers, perhaps using their own primer, a book in which they collected their own prayers, biblical stories and pictures. Such primers were expensive but not beyond the pocket of a successful merchant or professional soldier. The poorer worshipper would recite their Pater nosters and Ave Marias.

A great volume of the work produced by medieval artists was for the churches or about religious themes and, despite the ravages of the Reformation, some of this art is preserved for us today in a number of different mediums, in embroidery in the "opus anglicanum" so called because the English embroiderers were so good at it, in stained glass, in manuscript illuminations, in memorial brasses, in carved ivories, carved wooden panels and statues, in carved stone, in worked precious and non-precious metals making objects such as crucifixes and candlesticks, in enamelled plaques and in paintings on canvas, wood and plastered walls.

One very interesting facet of this religious art is that there appears to have been a fairly rigid format for each subject - the number of people in each scene, their position relative to each other, the direction in which they face and the position of their arms, legs and hands all seem to have been dictated by some central authority. However, rather than being laid down by religious authority like, for example, one of the controlling abbeys of the large Orders such as the Abbey of Bec, this iconography came from a school of artists in Paris, whence it appears to have spread throughout most of the western Christian church. So

that whether you see the picture embroidered on a stole or in a book, in a stained glass window or in a mural it is immediately recognizable as a particular scene, like, for instance, the Birth of Christ or the Adoration of the Magi. Occasionally the scenes are identical except that they are mirror images - were they copied from pinhole templates which got put the wrong way round ?

Our wall paintings then are not unique but where they have faded or have been covered over by later memorials we can at least guess quite accurately at what they are from similar scenes elsewhere. Examples of other sources for our pictures are given in the following descriptions wherever possible. The fact that these examples come from across Europe, from Italy to Norway, from Durham to Berlin, shows just how "universal" was the language of medieval religious iconography.

THE SCHEME

At Chalgrove we are very fortunate in having a nearly complete set of early 14th century wall paintings, which are all associated in some way with the Virgin Mary, to whom the church is dedicated. The paintings can be considered under four main headings: the Incarnation and Redemption of Jesus Christ with the sequel of the Death and Triumph of His mother the Virgin Mary, the Doom, and finally the individual Saints who adorn the window alcoves. The story runs from the descent of Christ from King David, in the Jesse Tree, right through to the Day of Judgement, or Doom, and has been arranged so that the two moments of triumph, the Ascension of Christ and the Coronation of Mary, are together on either side of the East Window.

Whilst the Life of Christ is a fairly common topic elsewhere, the story of the Virgin Mary is a rarity and particularly when almost complete as it is here. Surviving images of the Virgin throwing down her girdle to reassure St. Thomas are rare in this country. The Girdle itself is claimed as a great relic of Prato, 10 miles north west of Florence in Italy, and it is a popular subject in much medieval Italian art.

The selection of the Saints for the window alcoves also presents a puzzle for us. Saints Helen and Mary Magdalene are associated with the death and crucifixion of Jesus, John the Baptist and John the Evangelist are also closely associated with Jesus and Mary as are Saints Peter and Paul, but what is the link between Saints Bartholomew and Laurence and the Virgin? Perhaps it is simply that their Saints Days fall adjacent to Mary's Assumption in the calendar, or were they chosen because they were favourites, or namesakes of the Barentins or of the Vicar?. We are not helped by the destruction of the stained glass windows. The window splays were clearly set aside for figures of saints and we can see this elsewhere, for example in Nassington in Northamptonshire. The adjacent windows almost certainly continued the same theme, so in each window we now see only two of what was a group of four saints, two painted on the splays and two illuminated in stained glass.

Fortunately, when the paintings were re-discovered, they were faithfully sketched in great detail by Mr C.A.Buckler on 21st June 1859. We shall use these sketches alongside photographs and other illustrations to help in the explanation of the paintings. In the 1930s Professor E W Tristram, one of the leading authorities on wall paintings of his day, did some restoration work on the paintings and also made a number of very accurate drawings of them which he then published in his book "English Wallpaintings of the Fourteenth Century". We have also been very fortunate in having our paintings selected as the topic for his Master of Arts thesis by Mr Stephen Maynard, a student at the University of York Centre for Medieval Studies in 1986. I am indebted to him for a copy of his thesis and have used many of his conclusions in the following pages.

THE LIFE OF CHRIST

Being the more important of the two stories, this story is painted on the North Wall of the church. Unfortunately this means that it has suffered more erosion due to sunlight and the effects of salts in the plaster than have the paintings of the story of Mary on the opposite wall.

The story starts with the Jesse Tree at the bottom left of the wall, continues with the Annunciation Window to the right of the Jesse Tree, and the Nativity and the Adoration of the Magi to the right of that. Then in the next tier up, above the Nativity is the Slaughter of the Innocents, with the Presentation in the Temple to the right. Finally the Passion story runs across the top tier from left above the Jesse Tree to right and down the right hand side of the wall, moving in to the left hand side of paintings in the East wall with the Harrowing of Hell at the bottom and rising up to the Ascension at the top. The sequence of "reading" on all three tiers is from the West towards the East Window, i.e. from left to right as you face them.

Fig 9. The arrangement of the paintings on the North wall and the north side of the East wall.

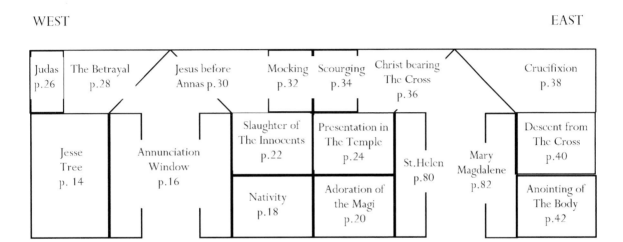

WEST   EAST

| Judas p.26 | The Betrayal p.28 | Jesus before Annas p.30 | Mocking p.32 | Scourging p.34 | Christ bearing The Cross p.36 | Crucifixion p.38 |

| Jesse Tree p. 14 | Annunciation Window p.16 | Slaughter of The Innocents p.22 | Presentation in The Temple p.24 | St.Helen p.80 | Mary Magdalene p.82 | Descent from The Cross p.40 |
| Nativity p.18 | Adoration of the Magi p.20 | Anointing of The Body p.42 |

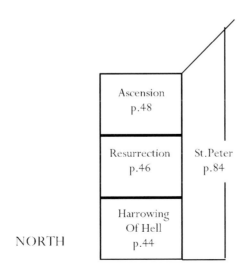

Ascension p.48	
Resurrection p.46	St.Peter p.84
Harrowing Of Hell p.44	

NORTH

Fig 10.

'Jesus was about thirty years old when he began his work. He was the son (as was thought) of Joseph son of Heli, son of Matthat, son of Levi, son of Melchi ... son of Nathan, son of David, son of Jesse ... son of Seth, son of Adam, son of God.' [Luke 3, 23 - 38]

THE JESSE TREE

This is a popular local theme with the magnificent stone window-tree in Dorchester Abbey and the extraordinary tree on the painted panel ceiling of St.Helen's Church in Abingdon. Our tree has two branches of the vine forming two oval compartments indicating the descent of the infant Jesus, held by Mary, in the top oval, from King David playing his harp in the bottom oval, (St.Matthew's Gospel chapter 1, verses 1 to 17).

Other Jesse trees usually have the recumbent figure of Jesse himself lying across the bottom of the picture. In his place we have some lines of script, now indecipherable, but which quite likely quoted the words of Isaiah 11 verse 1

'Et egredietur virga radice Jesse
et flos de radice ejus ascendit.'
['A shoot shall come out from the stump of Jesse, and a branch shall grow out of his roots']

The other feature to note in this scene is the figure of Mary herself, a young and really quite beautiful girl, fashionably dressed, carefully cradling her child who raises his hand in blessing. This typifies the attitude of the artist towards the Virgin which occurs throughout our paintings, an attitude which emphasises the humanity of Mary and which is one of the artist's most touching traits.

The carved wooden knife handle, now in the British Museum, shows Jesus sitting in judgement above King David playing his harp (fig.11).

Fig 11. The Jesse Tree as it appears today. Note the two lines of script running across the bottom centre of the picture.

Fig 12. The Jesse Tree carved in an English late 15th century wooden knife handle, now in the British Museum.

Fig 13.

'In the sixth month the angel Gabriel was sent by God to a town in Galilee called Nazareth, to a virgin engaged to a man whose name was Joseph, of the House of David. The virgin's name was Mary. And he came to her and said, "Greetings, favoured one! The Lord is with you." But she was much perplexed by his words and pondered what sort of greeting this might be. The angel said to her, "Do not be afraid, Mary, for you have found favour with God. And now, you will conceive in your womb and bear a son, and you will name him Jesus. He will be great, and will be called the Son of the Most High, and the Lord God will give to him the throne of his ancestor David. He will reign over the house of Jacob forever, and of his kingdom there will be no end." [Luke 1.26 - 33]

The Annunciation is the first of the five Joyful Mysteries.

THE ANNUNCIATION WINDOW

On either side of the window we have the figures of the Archangel Gabriel (left) and Mary (right) and the window shapes above their heads indicate that they were part of the whole window, the Annunciation being 'the window through which the Incarnation was made possible.' We do not know when our stained glass windows were destroyed, either by Edward VI's decree or by the Puritans of Cromwell's Commonwealth, but we can guess at what they contained from contemporary representations of the same scene.

From Gabriel's mouth curving down the left hand window would have been a speech banner bearing the words "Ave Maria, gratia plena...." (Hail Mary, full of grace...) or as many of them as the artist could fit in. In the right hand window at the bottom would have stood a pot from which a lily grew upwards in front of Mary, the lily being her symbol. Finally in the quatrefoil shaped window at the top would have been a dove representing the Holy Spirit. We can see all of these details in the picture below (fig.15) of part of an opus anglicanum embroidery Orphrey of the early fourteenth century. This was executed in silver and silver-gilt thread with underside couching, coloured silks in split stitch and couched work on velvet, and can be seen in the Victoria and Albert Museum. What a colourful picture the whole of our annunciation window would have been !

The mediaeval theologians had solved the riddle of the virgin birth by deciding that the Holy Spirit had entered into Mary to achieve the conception through her ear when she heard the Annunciation, and so this is depicted in our "window" by three short lines pointing into Mary's right ear.

Fig 14. The paintings as they now appear either side of the North West window

Fig 15. The Annunciation in embroidery, from an early 14th Century English orphrey, now in the Victoria & Albert Museum

Fig 16.

'While they were there, the time came for her to deliver her child. And she gave birth to her firstborn son and wrapped him in bands of cloth, and laid him in a manger, because there was no place for them in the inn.' [Luke 2.6 - 7]

THE NATIVITY

This painting has suffered most from the ravages of time and we have to refer to Mr Buckler's sketch and to other versions of this scene to understand what it probably contained.

We can just make out Mary on the left lying on a couch and some of the drapery is still visible. On the right Joseph sits at the foot of the couch. The figures in the centre background are now completely gone but Buckler's sketch shows a lady, the Christ child and a disembodied hand. In the apocryphal Gospel of Pseudo-Matthew, Joseph fetched two midwives, Zelomi and Salome, to the birth of Jesus. Zelomi believed but Salome was incredulous and so her hand withered until it was cured by touching the swaddling cloth. It is possible then that the central figures shown by Buckler were Zelomi and the Christ child with the hand of Salome.

One representation of this scene can be seen in the painted wooden roof of the church in Aal in Norway, which is reproduced here (fig.18). Nearer to Chalgrove is the wallpainting in St.Clement's Church at Ashampstead, south of the River Thames near Wallingford (fig.19).

The Nativity is the third of the five Joyful Mysteries.

Fig 17. The Nativity scene as it is now

Fig 18. Scene from the painted roof of the wooden church in Aal, Norway, a copy of the original dating from c.1250 AD. The characters' positions are the same as in our painting, but there are an "ox and an ass" extra and only one midwife.

Fig 19 The Nativity scene in the wall painting in St.Clement's Church, Ashampstead in Berkshire. The midwife is next to Joseph at the foot of the crib.

Fig 20.

'In the time of King Herod, after Jesus was born in Bethlehem of Judea, wise men from the East came to Jerusalem, asking, "Where is the child who has been born king of the Jews? For we observed his star at its rising, and have come to pay him homage."… and there ahead of them went the star … until it stopped over the place where the child was. When they saw that the star had stopped, they were overwhelmed with joy. On entering the house, they saw the child with Mary his mother; and they knelt down and paid him homage. Then, opening their treasure chests, they offered him gifts of gold, frankincense, and myrrh.'
[Matthew 2.1 - 11]

THE ADORATION OF THE MAGI

This scene is also now almost completely lost but again we can see its composition from Mr Buckler's sketch and from contemporary works. Mary on the left holds Jesus on her lap. One of the three Kings kneels before them to present his gift, while the other two Kings stand on the right facing each other.

Comparing Buckler's sketch with the carved ivory French Diptych from the second half of the 14th century, which is now in the British Museum (fig.22), we see that one is very nearly the mirror image of the other. There are differences in the way the third King is holding his arms but these are probably due to Buckler's interpretation of what was rather difficult to make out.

The same general scene is shown on the Byzantine Gold Medallion from the British Museum (fig.23), which dates from the 6th or 7th century AD, some six or seven hundred years before our wallpaintings !

Fig 21. The Adoration of the Magi as it appears today

Fig 22. The scene from the 14th C carved ivory French Diptych, now in the British Museum. See also fig 65 on page 47.

Fig 23. Byzantine Gold medallion, now in the British Museum

Fig 24.

'When Herod saw that he had been tricked by the wise men, he was infuriated, and he sent and killed all the children in and around Bethlehem who were two years old or under, according to the time that he had learned from the wise men.' [Matthew 2.16]

THE SLAUGHTER OF THE INNOCENTS

Much of this grisly scene is missing, but it is our first introduction to the artist's partiality for showing copious gouts of blood ! King Herod sits on a throne on the left facing a spear on which is impaled a baby boy, dripping blood. The spear is held by a soldier no longer visible behind whom there were possibly two other cameos, first a mother struggling with a soldier over a murdered child - she trying to pluck out one of the soldier's eyes - each of them grasping one of the child's arms, and second a distressed mother holding her dead child. This is the typical sequence for depicting this topic as is shown (again in mirror image from our picture) in the embroidered fragment of a late fourteenth century English orphrey (border of an ecclesiastical garment), fig 26, which is now in the V&A Museum.

Fig 25. The Slaughter of the Innocents. Note the child impaled on the spear.

Fig 26. This fragment of an embroidered orphrey dates from the late 14th Century and is a mirror image of our wall painting, except that King Herod is not shown. Again note the child impaled on the spear or sword in the same relative position as in the painting.

Fig 27.

'When the time came for their purification according to the law of Moses, they brought him up to Jerusalem to present him to the Lord....and they offered a sacrifice...a pair of turtledoves or two young pigeons...Guided by the Spirit, Simeon came into the temple; and when the parents brought in the child Jesus, to do for him what was customary under the law, Simeon took him in his arms and praised God, saying "Master, now you are dismissing your servant in peace, according to your word; for my eyes have seen your salvation ..." ...There was also a prophet, Anna the daughter of Phanuel, of the tribe of Asher ... At that moment she came, and began to praise God and to speak about the child to all who were looking for the redemption of Jerusalem.' [Luke 2.22 - 38]

THE PRESENTATION IN THE TEMPLE

Of this section of four pictures of the childhood of Jesus, this painting is the best preserved. Simeon on the right of the altar stretches out his hand in blessing to Jesus, who is held out to him by Mary. Behind Mary stands Anna the prophetess, and beside her is a second figure. We might expect this to be Joseph and, while this person might at first glance appear to be female, he clearly has a beard. Usually in this scene Joseph, or Anna, is shown carrying a basket of doves, but if this was included in our painting it has long since disappeared. The picture in the Laud manuscript (c.1380 - c.1400), fig 29, has the same layout as ours, but with Anna and doves, and no Joseph.

The Presentation in the Temple is the fourth of the five Joyful Mysteries.

Fig 28. The Presentation in the Temple

Fig 29. The Presentation from the Laud Manuscript in the Bodleian Library.

THE PASSION OF CHRIST

The Passion story runs across the top of the North wall and appears to follow the story as told in Saint John's Gospel, chapters 13 to 19.

'After saying this Jesus was troubled in spirit, and declared, "Very truly, I tell you, one of you will betray me."… One of his disciples … asked him, "Lord, who is it?" Jesus answered, "It is the one to whom I give this piece of bread when I have dipped it in the dish." So when he had dipped the piece of bread, he gave it to Judas son of Simon Iscariot. After he received the bread, Satan entered into him. Jesus said to him, "Do quickly what you are going to do" … So after receiving the piece of bread, he immediately went out. And it was night.' [John 13, 21- 30]

JUDAS

The story starts in the West (left hand as you face it) corner with an unidentifiable scene (fig. 31) of which only the right hand figure remains, headless and in ochre robes facing into the corner. In all of the scenes on our walls the characters face inwards towards each other and the clue as to which way they are facing is given by the lines of their clothes. This ochre figure then was on the right hand side of a small scene with one or perhaps a couple of other figures. C A Buckler's sketches of 1859 do not show this figure and it only really became visible during the restoration work on the North wall in 1986. Assuming that the now blank West wall above the chancel arch once held a magnificent painting of the Last Supper, (this is a wild guess on my part with no supporting evidence except that it is an obvious place for such a picture, there being such a scene in this position in the church of Strangnas in Sweden and also at Fairsteads church in Essex, fig. 30), then the mystery scene could have been either Judas receiving the silver, or Jesus' agony in the garden. However, we know that yellow is the colour of treachery and so it is probably Judas who is portrayed here receiving his silver. The carved ivory in the French Diptych from the Soissons group (fig. 32) shows the three scenes of Judas' betrayal and the first scene matches the position of this scene here.

Fig 30. The painted wall across the chancel arch in the church at Fairsteads in Essex. At the top Christ enters Jerusalem on a donkey, while a child in the tree cuts down branches to throw before him. Below this, the Last Supper is on the left and the Betrayal on the right. The two figures in the centre, below the tree, are part of the Betrayal scene

Fig 31. The scene on the North West wall to the left of the Betrayal

Fig 32. Part of the carved ivory French Soissons Diptych from the end of the 13th century showing Judas' betrayal. Note the three scenes - Judas receives the silver, left, kisses Jesus, centre, and hangs disembowelled from a tree, right. See also page 55.

Fig 33.

'So Judas brought a detachment of soldiers together with police from the chief priests and the Pharisees, and they came there with lanterns and torches and weapons. Then Jesus, knowing all that was to happen to him, came forward and asked them, "Whom are you looking for?" They replied "Jesus of Nazareth." Jesus replied, "I am he."... Then Simon Peter, who had a sword, drew it, struck the high priest's slave, and cut off his right ear. The slave's name was Malchus.' [John 18.3 - 10]

THE BETRAYAL

To the right of Judas is the scene depicting Judas' kiss of betrayal. On the left hand side we see Peter in a dark mantle with his left hand raised to stop the arrest of Jesus, while with the sword in his right hand he casually lops off the ear of Malchus, the High Priest's servant. Malchus appears to be kneeling and is much smaller than Peter, and of course there are copious gouts of blood flowing from his ear !

To the right of Peter and Malchus, Judas reaches across the front of Jesus to embrace him and plant the traitor's kiss. Behind them, and to the right are other figures who were possibly soldiers (there is a fist grasping the handle of a spear) and apostles. Alternatively in this position, on the extreme right hand side of the scene could have been Judas hanging from his traitors tree with his guts spilling out, as in the carved ivory Soissons Diptych (fig. 32 and page 55).

The three central subjects of Peter and Malchus, the kiss of betrayal and the arrest of Jesus form the content of most versions of this scene. A typical manuscript version comes from the collection of canticles, hymns and the Passion of Christ, c.1280 to c.1290, fig. 35, originating from St.Augustine's at Canterbury and now owned by St.John's College, Cambridge.

Fig 34. The Betrayal

Fig 35. Picture of the Betrayal from the manuscript collection from St. Augustine's Canterbury, now owned by St. John's College, Cambridge

Fig 36.

'So the soldiers, their officer, and the Jewish police arrested Jesus and bound him. First they took him to Annas, who was the father-in-law of Caiaphas, the high priest that year.' [John 18.12 - 13]

JESUS BEFORE ANNAS

On the other side of the top of the window arch we see Jesus brought before Annas. I had previously thought that the "judge" in this picture was Pilate but Stephen Maynard points out quite correctly that if the sequence of pictures follows the story narrated in the gospels then this picture must show Jesus before either Caiaphas or Annas, the latter being most likely the subject of our painting, as this incident gets more verses in John's version of the story than does the visit to Caiaphas.

Annas, seated on the window arch, wears a cap and raises his right hand in accusation, while Jesus to the right of him is held between two servants.

The comparable version of the picture, from the Gough Psalter, fig 38, is in reverse of our version and raises once again who is the judge as it is entitled 'Christ before Caiaphas'. A similar picture in the Sarum Hours, c.1340 to c.1350, now owned by Trinity College, Dublin, is entitled 'Christ before Pilate' as was our sketch by Mr Buckler.

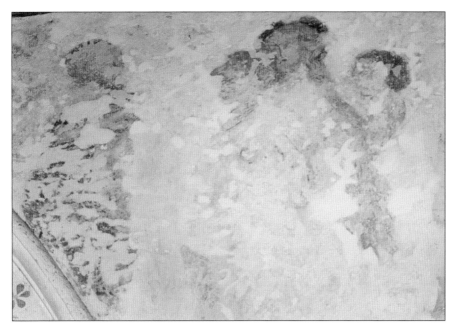

Fig 37. Jesus before Annas

Fig 38. "Christ before Caiaphas" from the Gough Psalter

Fig 39.

'And the soldiers wove a crown of thorns and put it on his head, and they dressed him in a purple robe. They kept coming up to him, saying, "Hail, King of the Jews!" and striking him on the face'
[John 19.2 - 3]

THE MOCKING BY THE JEWS

Very little remains of this scene, which is of a fairly standard composition. Christ is blindfolded and stands between two people. The one on the left looks up and sticks out his tongue, while the one on the right appears to be laughing and wears a conical shaped "Jews" hat with a very long curly point. There are in fact traces of two other people in the picture, above and "behind" the two that we can see, with a hand apparently tugging at Jesus' hair. Jesus' bound hands are shown in Buckler's sketch but are now barely visible.

A comparable scene in an enamelled plaque from the French Limoges workshop of Nardon Pericaud (dated circa 1520), fig. 42, shows the scene more clearly. Christ seated wears the crimson robe and crown of thorns while two people kneel to him and two others are hitting him with reeds.

The scene from the wallpaintings of the church in Glamorgan, fig. 41, which were discovered shortly before the derelict building was demolished, and which are now in the Welsh Folk Museum at St.Fagans near Cardiff, show two people spitting at Jesus which is probably what the characters in our wallpainting were doing.

The Crowning with Thorns is the second of the five Sorrowful Mysteries.

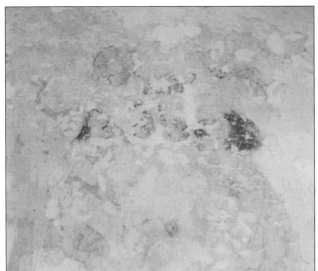

Fig 40. The Mocking as it appears today

Fig 41. The fragment of wallpainting from a Glamorgan church , now in the Welsh Folk Museum

Fig 42. The French enamel plaque, circa 1520AD, from the Limoges Worshop, now in the Fitzwilliam Museum in Cambridge, clearly shows the full picture

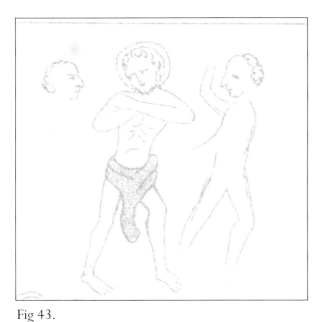

Fig 43.

'Then Pilate took Jesus and had him flogged.' [John 19.1]

THE SCOURGING OF JESUS

The next cameo scene is also composed of three figures. Again Christ is in the centre, his bound hands held across his chest, presumably tied to a vertical post of which there is no trace. He wears just a cloth around his loins and is dotted with black specks representing blood. The heads of his two assailants are visible on either side and above the one on the left can be clearly seen his two fists grasping the scourge to be brought down across Jesus' back.

The opus anglicanum version of this scene shown below, fig. 45, comes from the orphrey (border) of a chasuble (sleeveless cloak worn by a priest at the eucharist) dated to the early fourteenth century, in other words contemporary with our paintings. It shows Jesus in a similar sort of stance with his head facing left forwards and wrapped around the post to which he is tied. The bespattered specks of blood are there and the two-handed method of using the scourge.

It is not clear whether or not our painting had the scourging post. There is no sign of it at all either above or below Jesus' head, and as some artists adopted the idea of placing the post behind Jesus while showing him in the same position as if he was tied to a post in front of him, as in the picture from the Gough manuscript, fig. 46, it is possible that this idea has been used here.

The Scourging at the Pillar is the third of the five Sorrowful Mysteries.

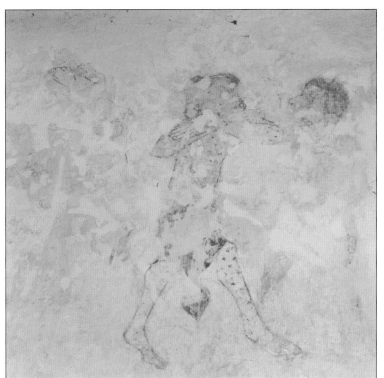

Fig 44. The Scourging-note the raised hands holding the whip top left and the drops of blood on Jesus' legs.

Fig 45. 'Opus anglicanum' embroidery orphrey showing the Scourging.

Fig 46. The same scene from the Gough Psalter

Fig 47.

'Then he handed him over to them to be crucified. So they took Jesus; and carrying the cross by himself, he went out to what is called The Place of the Skull, which in Hebrew is called Golgotha.' [John 19.16 - 17]

CHRIST BEARING THE CROSS

In the same way as our artist has Annas leaning against the window slope to cross-examine Jesus, so in this scene he uses the rising slope of the next window to represent the hill of Calvary. A man carrying a bucket, containing presumably the hammer and nails, leads Jesus up this hill. Jesus carries the cross over his right shoulder and is followed by other figures. He looks backwards but Buckler's sketch does not show his mother Mary behind him. This was certainly the case in the Gough Psalter version of the picture, as shown below, fig 49, and the photograph of the wall painting as it is today, fig 48, shows a shadowy female figure at the left hand side which could well have been Mary.

The Carrying of the Cross is the fourth of the five Sorrowful Mysteries.

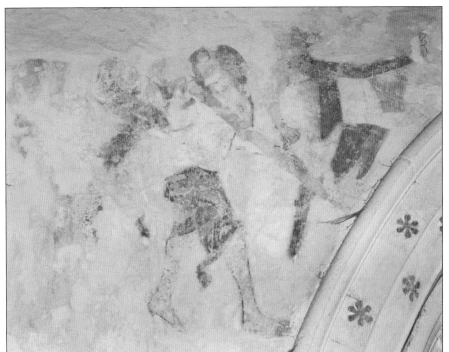

Fig 48. Christ bearing the Cross

Fig 49. Again the manuscript Gough Psalter in the Bodleian Library shows a very similar scene

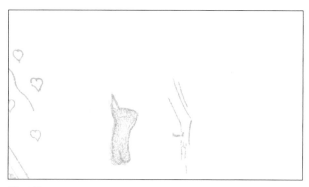

Fig 50.

'There they crucified him ... Meanwhile standing near the cross of Jesus were his mother, and his mother's sister, Mary the wife of Clopas, and Mary Magdalene ... So they put a sponge full of the wine on a branch of hyssop and held it to his mouth. When Jesus had received the wine, he said, "It is finished." Then he bowed his head and gave up his spirit ... But when they came to Jesus and saw that he was already dead, they did not break his legs. Instead, one of the soldiers pierced his side with a spear, and at once blood and water came out.' [John 19.18 - 34]

THE CRUCIFIXION

Unfortunately we have lost the great majority of this picture. Buckler's sketch gave very little information, just a torso and part of Jesus' foot. Fortunately, as with other small details like the two-handed scourge mentioned above, the restoration of the North Wall in 1986 revealed quite a bit more. The torso turns out to be a little man hammering the nail into Jesus' feet which are spurting more gouts of blood. Behind the hammerer are the shadowy remains of a figure, while on the other side of Jesus' feet are a pair of dark legs and behind them another hand and a leg.

The Passion scene from the Trinity College manuscript (Fig 52) gives us an idea of the probable composition of this scene. The little man is busy with hammer and nail at the bottom centre, the man on the right holds the bucket in one hand while proffering the sponge on the hyssop stick to Jesus' lips, and the man on the left behind the hammerer sticks the lance into Jesus' side. So once again we have three cameos in the one picture. What a pity we have lost most of it !

The Crucifixion is the fifth of the five Sorrowful Mysteries.

Fig 51. What remains of the Crucifixion scene

Fig 52. The Crucifixion scene from the Trinity College manuscript.

Fig 53.

'After these things, Joseph of Arimathea, who was a disciple of Jesus, though a secret one because of his fear of the Jews, asked Pilate to let him take away the body of Jesus. Pilate gave him permission; so he came and removed his body.' [John 19.38]

THE DESCENT FROM THE CROSS

This is one of the better preserved paintings on the North Wall and gives us a good idea of what the previous picture must have looked like. In the centre, Christ hangs lifeless, his weight supported by Joseph of Arimathea (centre left) and Nicodemus (centre right standing) while a servant kneeling (centre right) removes the nail from Jesus' feet. On the left of the picture the grieving Mary tenderly kisses Jesus' tortured arm, while on the right stands Saint John whom Jesus "made" Mary's son from the Cross (St. John chapter 19 verses 26 and 27). Jesus' wounds in hands, feet and side are obviously shown in the artist's characteristic way, but this picture is also an excellent example of the freedom of style and composition which our artist gave to all our paintings and also of the tender reverence in which he represents Mary throughout the whole scheme.

The Gough Psalter has a very similar composition of this scene (Fig 55). The same scene can also be seen in the Jonsberg altar piece , see page 83, and the Soissons Diptych on page 55.

Fig 54. The Descent from the Cross

Fig 55. The same scene from the Gough Psalter

41

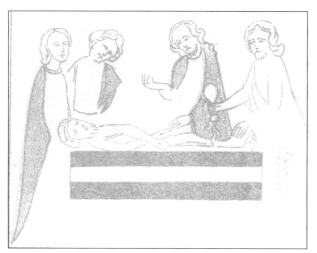

Fig 56.

'Nicodemus, who had first come to Jesus by night, also came, bringing a mixture of myrrh and aloes, weighing about a hundred pounds. They took the body of Jesus and wrapped it with the spices in linen cloths, according to the burial custom of the Jews. Now there was a garden in the place where he was crucified, and in the garden there was a new tomb in which no one had ever been laid. And so, because it was the Jewish day of Preparation, and the tomb was nearby, they laid Jesus there.' [John 19.39 - 42]

THE ANOINTING OF THE BODY

This scene was previously identified as 'The Entombment', but in medieval iconography that is a different picture and our painting is correctly identified by Stephen Maynard as 'The Anointing of the Body'.

All the characters from the previous scene are here. On the left Joseph of Arimethea cradles Jesus' head in his hands, while next to him Mary bows her head in mourning. No longer visible, Saint John kneels in front of Mary but behind the slab on which Jesus lies. Next to him Nicodemus holds a bottle of ointment in his right hand (the bottle has disappeared too) and holds Jesus' hand in his left hand. Next to him the servant pours oil from a bottle on to Jesus' body.

A lot of this scene is lost or indistinct and we have to rely on Buckler's sketch and a similar picture from the Gough Psalter (Fig.58) to see what it really was like.

Fig 57. The Anointing of the Body

Fig 58. The Gough Psalter's version of the picture shows us what has been lost from our wallpainting

Fig 59.

'And the Lord stretched forth his hand and made the sign of the cross over Adam and over all his saints, and he took the right hand of Adam and went up out of hell, and all the saints followed him.' [Acts of Pilate p.139 The Apochryphal New Testament by M R James]

We now move to the bottom of the East Wall on the left hand side for the next scene which is called

THE HARROWING OF HELL

Jesus stands on the left rather nonchalantly holding a staff (probably the vexillum but the cross piece and pennant are no longer visible) with his right hand and leading with his left hand Adam and Eve and the souls of the just from the jaws of hell, represented by a gaping serpent's jaws. Unfortunately, whilst Buckler's drawing clearly shows the serpent's jaws, they have by now faded from view, all except for one large fang which thrusts up between Adam's legs. The picture signifies Christ's victory over Satan and the powers of Hell, and the freeing of the pre-Incarnation just from their bonds. The picture from the Gough Psalter (Fig 61) is more elaborate but shows similar positioning of the figures. A similar, but later, picture from a painted reredos in Saint Maurice Cathedral in Angers, France, (Fig 61) has Jesus and the jaws of hell in the same positions as ours.

Note also the line of inscription across the top of this scene. This is dealt with fully on page 76.

Fig 60. The Harrowing of Hell. Note the upturned fang of Hell's jaws in the centre between the legs of the central character

Fig 61. The 15th century painted reredos in Saint Maurice Cathedral in Angers, France, showing the Harrowing of Hell

Fig 62. The same scene from the Gough Psalter

Fig 63.

'... an angel of the Lord, descending from heaven, came and rolled back the stone and sat on it ... For fear of him the guards shook and became like dead men. But the angel said to the women, "Do not be afraid; I know that you are looking for Jesus who was crucified. He is not here; for he has been raised, as he said ... " Suddenly Jesus met them and said "Greetings!" And they came to him, took hold of his feet and worshipped him.'
[Matthew, chapter 28, verses 2 to 9]

THE RESURRECTION

This picture is immediately above the Harrowing of Hell. It shows Christ, once again wearing a cloak, rising from the tomb with the vexillum in his left hand, while he raises his right hand in blessing. Two angels escort him and three Roman soldiers sleep on undisturbed, underneath the arches. The signs of His crucifixion, the stigmata, are clearly visible in Christ's side, hands and feet. The tomb is shown as a typical medieval tomb such as can be seen locally in Dorchester Abbey, or Christchurch Cathedral in Oxford, and not as a rock tomb with a stone rolled away from its mouth which we now understand it to have been.

The picture is a standard representation of this important scene which can be seen in many contemporary manuscripts, for example the Gough Psalter in the Bodleian Library. The French carved ivory diptych in the British Museum (Fig 65) has an almost identical picture but without the arches and Roman soldiers. See also the Soissons Diptych on page 55.

The Resurrection is the first of the five Glorious Mysteries.

Fig 64. The Resurrection. Note the Roman soldiers asleep underneath the arches.

Fig 65. The Resurrection from the French ivory Diptych c.1350AD now in the British Museum. See also the Soissons Diptych on page 55.

Fig 66.

'Then he led them out as far as Bethany, and, lifting up his hands, he blessed them. While he was blessing them, he withdrew from them and was carried up into heaven.' [Luke 24.50]

THE ASCENSION

The final scene in the life of Christ is above the Resurrection scene and shows the Virgin Mary and the Apostles watching as Christ's feet and the bottom of his cloak disappear above them into the clouds. St. Peter carrying the keys is clearly visible standing behind Mary.

Again this is a fairly "standard" representation of this scene, but there are subtle differences compared with the picture from the Gough Psalter shown here. For example Mary's hands are clasped together in prayer in our picture, and the Apostles are more crowded than in the two rows shown in the Gough Psalter (Fig 68).

As the wall paintings and stained glass windows would have formed a single scheme, it is possible that the East window of the church would have contained a representation of Christ in Glory, this being the culmination of the Life of Christ.

The Ascension is the second of the five Glorious Mysteries.

Fig 67. The Ascension as it is today.

Fig 68. The Ascension from the Gough Psalter

Turning now to the South Wall, what strikes us immediately is how much better preserved these paintings are. This is probably due to two reasons, firstly the sun does not fall on them causing them to fade, and secondly they were treated by Eve Baker using modern conservation techniques some ten years before the North Wall was treated.

There are three "stories" on the South Wall, the "Doom" or Last Judgement on the right hand side, the Death and Assumption of the Virgin Mary and the story of Saint Thomas and the Girdle.

THE DEATH AND ASSUMPTION OF MARY

As the early church developed after the Resurrection, there were not a few deviations and heresies, and inevitably besides the Gospels of Matthew, Mark, Luke and John there were other stories written down which purported to be about true happenings but which were, for the most part, fanciful inventions. These are known as the apocryphal gospels and have appeared in different forms throughout the ages, including some of the medieval Mystery Plays. The modern student can read them in M.R. James' excellent book 'The Apocryphal New Testament', but at the time of our wall-paintings you would have had to read the Narrative of Joseph of Arimathea about the Assumption of the Blessed Virgin Mary or the Golden Legend by Jacobus de Voragine, the Archbishop of Genoa from 1292 to 1298, who took a number of the apocryphal writings and put them together in his book which was later printed by Caxton. You might also have heard and seen the story portrayed in a Mystery Play.

Our wallpaintings of The Death and Assumption of Mary, whilst in generally better condition than the Life of Christ on the opposite wall, have suffered during their hidden years from having two massive marble memorials placed on top of them. I am often asked if there are likely to be the remains of the paintings behind the memorials but I fear that most of the plaster, and therefore paintings, will have been removed so that the memorials could be set into and held securely by the wall.

Again the sequence of "reading" on all three tiers is from the West towards the East window, except that for the moment we ignore the painting to the West of the Westernmost South window, the Doom (see pages 79 to 81).

Fig 69. The arrangement of the wall paintings on the south wall and the south side of the east wall.

EAST   WEST

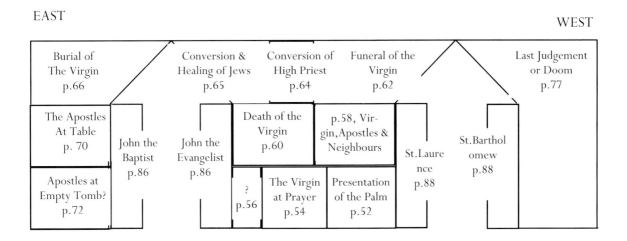

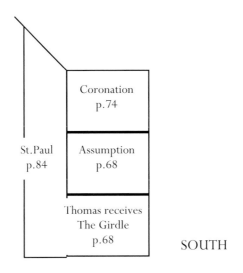

SOUTH

51

Fig 70.

'One day the Virgin's heart was aflame with desire to be with her Son; she was so deeply stirred in spirit that her tears flowed abundantly. She could not with serenity of soul bear his being taken away for a time and the loss of his consoling presence. Then behold, an angel stood before her amid a great light and greeted her reverently as the mother of his Lord. "Hail, blessed Mary!" he said, "receive the blessing of him who bestowed salvation on Jacob. See, Lady, I have brought you a palm branch from paradise, and you are to have it carried before your bier. Three days from now you will be assumed from the body, because your Son is waiting for you, his venerable mother.' [The Golden Legend Vol.2,p.78]

THE PRESENTATION OF THE PALM

The story begins when the Angel (right) brings Mary the Palm of Paradise and announces that the hour approaches for her re-union with her Divine Son. Behind Mary to our left there are some black drapes, which are in fact Mary's blue gown which she has removed so that she can wear the pink coloured "clothes of immortality" brought for her by the Angel.

In the carved ivory plaque by the Master of Kremsmunster on the Upper Rhine, dated to the last years of the 14th Century (Fig 72), we see in the top left hand corner the presentation of the palm.

In later representations of this scene, particularly in some Italian masterpieces, the Annunciation and the Presentation of the Palm become almost the same and are only distinguishable by seeing if it is a lily or a palm leaf which the Angel is giving to Mary.

Fig 71. The Presentation of the Palm of Paradise

Fig 72. Presentation of the Palm from the carved ivory diptych by the Master of Kremsmunster. See also page 93 for the complete diptych.

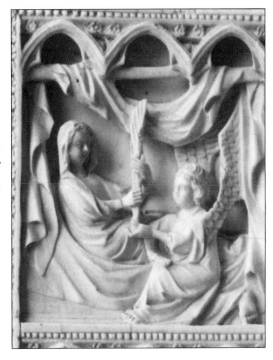

Fig 73.

'Then Mary put off her garments and clothed herself in her best raiment, and taking the palm which she had received of the angel's hand she went out into the Mount of Olivet and began to pray and to say: ....I pray thee, O king of glory, that no power of hell may hurt me....' [The Assumption:Latin narrative of Pseudo-Melito from The Apochryphal New Testament by M R James]

THE VIRGIN AT PRAYER

The second scene in the sequence then, shows Mary kneeling in prayer, wearing the pink robe, facing towards our left and with a blessing hand floating in the air above her head. Here the Virgin is praying to be preserved from the sight of the Evil One at the moment of her death. The dark blue robe she has removed hangs behind her - she has replaced her mortal robes with the "robes of immortality."

Although there are many pictures showing the hand of God coming out of a cloud in blessing, I have not yet found another one which shows this particular scene.

Fig 74. Mary praying - the scene as it is now

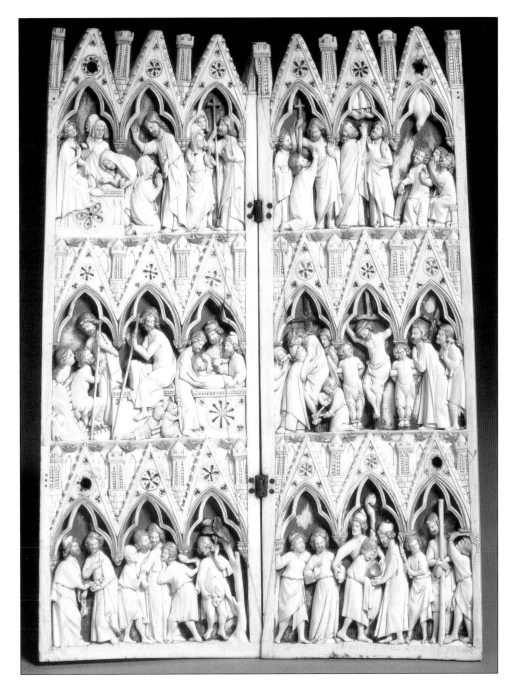

Fig. 75 The Soissons Diptych. Scenes from The Passion of Christ; ivory, painted and gilt; French (Paris); late 13th century. V & A Museum.

Fig 76.

'Now it happened that John was preaching in Ephesus when suddenly there was a clap of thunder, and a shining cloud picked him up and whisked him to Mary's door. He knocked and went in, and the virgin reverently greeted the Virgin. Seeing him, Mary was so astonished and happy that she could not contain her tears for joy..'
[The Golden Legend Vol 2,p.78]

UNKNOWN SCENE

The third picture is mostly obscured by the memorial to the Rev'd Francis Markham, who was Vicar at the time of the Restoration of the Monarchy and who died shortly afterwards in 1668. All that remains of the painting shows two ladies on the left, one wearing noticeably medieval headgear, and part of a figure on the right facing towards them. In the sequence of the story from the Golden Legend, Mary presents the Palm from Paradise to Saint John the Evangelist, and in fact right next to this painting, in the window splay, we see Saint John holding the Palm (see page 88) So it seems quite likely that this painting originally showed Mary with handmaidens on the left handing the Palm to John on the right. Either that or it is again a mirror image picture of the one in the top tier of the carved ivory plaque by the Master of Kremsmunster, to the right of the presentation of the palm, where Mary is showing the palm to her neighbours (Fig.78).

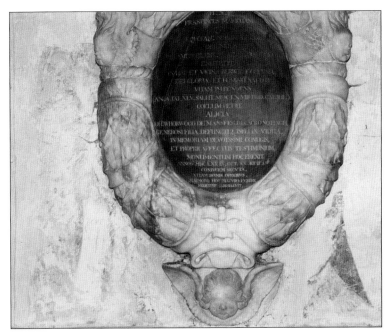

Fig 77. The scene covered by the Markham Memorial

Fig 78. Mary shows the palm to her handmaids, from the Master of Kremsmunster's carved ivory. Is this what our wallpainting looked like? See also page 93 for the complete diptych.

Fig 79.

'"Oh!" said John, "if only all my brother apostles were here to prepare proper obsequies for you and pay the honours you deserve!" Even as he was speaking, all the apostles were snatched up into the clouds from wherever they were preaching, and deposited at Mary's door..."
[The Golden Legend Vol.2,p.79]

THE VIRGIN, HER NEIGHBOURS AND THE APOSTLES

The next picture in the sequence is immediately above the presentation of the palm, in the centre tier, and shows Mary in the centre with the apostles to the left facing her and six female "neighbours" behind her. The story tells us that wherever the apostles were, and whether they were alive or dead, they were all miraculously transported to where Mary was - we see them all seated except for one, probably Saint John, who stands behind the foremost apostle who is probably Saint Peter (as he is tonsured). The neighbours gathered to Mary also and are represented here by six female figures, three standing and three kneeling in front of them. The foremost standing figure has long dark hair and may be Mary Magdelene. Note the headdresses of three of them, one has a veil and wimple and two have bands about their heads together with barbettes and crespines. All have their hands clasped in prayer. It has been suggested that, if the de Barantyn family did sponsor these wallpaintings, then some of these women may represent members of the de Barantyn family.

I have found no direct equivalent of this painting, the nearest (fig.81) being from the Italian painter Duccio di Buoninsegna (c.1260 - 1318), whose series of paintings called the Maesta are now in the Municipal Museum in Sienna. The Apostles on the left hand side of both paintings are similar but that is all.

Fig 80. Mary, the Apostles left and the neighbours right.

Fig 81.
Mary takes leave of the Apostles from Duccio's Maesta, now in the Municipal Museum in Sienna.

Fig 82.

'About the third hour of the night Jesus came with companies of angels, troops of prophets, hosts of martyrs, a legion of confessors and choirs of virgins, and all took their places before the Virgin's throne and sang dulcet canticles...Then Mary's soul went forth from her body and flew to the arms of her Son...' [The Golden Legend Vol.2,p79 - 80]

THE DEATH OF THE VIRGIN

To the left of the previous picture we see the death of Mary. The angels are clearly visible on the left but we have lost most of Mary because of the Markham memorial. The apostles are on the right and Mary lies on her deathbed across the centre, while behind her body we see her soul escorted by two angels rising to heaven. Again this scene is represented in the bottom row of the carved ivory plaque by the Master of Kremsmünster (Fig.85) in mirror image, and we also see it in the Italian manuscript (Fig.84) where Mary's soul is shown like a small baby wrapped in swaddling bands.

Fig 83. The Death of the Virgin Mary, partly obscured by the top of the Markham memorial

Fig 84. The scene from an Italian manuscript.

Fig 85. The Master of Kremsmunster's representation of the scene. See also page 93 for the complete diptych.

Fig 86.

'Then the apostles reverently lifted the body and placed it on a bier. ..., Peter and Paul then lifted the bier and Peter began to sing ... the other apostles took up the chant ... Angels were present too, singing with the apostles ... The populace was excited ... and came rushing out of the city to see what was going on. Then someone said: "The disciples of Jesus are carrying Mary away dead, and singing around her the melody you hear." At once they hurried to take arms and exhorted each other saying: "Come on, let us kill all those disciples and burn the body that bore the seducer." The chief priest ... said: "Look at the tabernacle of that man who disturbed us and our people so much! Look at the glory that is now paid to that woman!" After saying this he put his hands on the litter, intending to overturn it and throw the corpse to the ground. But suddenly his hands withered and stuck to the bier, so that he was hanging by his hands; and he moaned and cried in great pain, while the rest of the people were stricken with blindness by angels .'
[The Golden Legend Vol.2,p.81]

THE FUNERAL OF THE VIRGIN

This scene is above the neighbours and apostles scene, and shows the funeral procession. At the front is Saint John the Evangelist carrying the Palm, leading two groups of apostles who carry Mary's coffin by means of two poles on their shoulders. The coffin is draped with an elaborately patterned cloth and is surmounted at each end with a cross.

In the centre of the scene we see three small "Jewish" figures all suffering from their contact with the bier.

Our picture is a fairly standard representation of this scene, and part of a similar version can be seen in the church at Croughton in Northamptonshire.

The manuscript picture shown below (Fig.88) comes from Queen Mary's Psalter, now in the British Library. A similar scene can be seen on the embroidered Syon cope in the Victoria and Albert Museum (Fig.89), see also page 92.

Fig 87. The Funeral Procession of the Virgin.

Fig 88. The funeral procession in Queen Mary's Psalter, now in the British Library

Fig 89. The same scene from the Syon Cope

Fig 90.

'The chief priest cried out: "Holy Peter, do not scorn me in this extremity! Pray the Lord for me, I beg of you! You must remember how I stood by you and defended you when the portress accused you." Peter answered: "..if you believe in our Lord Jesus Christ and in this woman who conceived and bore him, I hope you will quickly receive the benefit of health." The chief priest said: "I believe that the Lord Jesus is the true Son of God, and that this woman was his most holy mother." At once his hands were loosed from the bier, but his arms were still withered and the pain was as severe as before. Peter told him: "Kiss the bier and say, 'I believe in Jesus Christ God, whom this woman carried in her womb and remained a virgin after she delivered her child.'" He did as he was told and was cured instantly.' [The Golden Legend Vol.2,p81]

CONVERSION OF THE HIGH PRIEST

This is the small two-character picture to the left of the previous one. The High Priest kneels in front of Saint John the Evangelist who holds the Palm of Paradise in one hand while with the other he sprinkles holy water over the High Priest using an aspergillum (wand).

As with Mary praying, page 54, I have been unable to find any other representations of this scene or the next, the Conversion and Healing of the Blinded Jews, page 65. Fortunately these two scenes are in fairly good condition, which is a good thing if, indeed, they are as rare as they appear to be.

Fig 91. Saint John the Evangelist converts the Prince of the Jews.

Fig 92.

'Peter then told him: "Take the palm from the hand of our brother John and hold it up over the people who have been blinded. Those who are willing to believe will receive their sight, those who refuse will never see again."'
[The Golden Legend Vol.2, p.81]

CONVERSION AND HEALING OF THE BLINDED JEWS

This is a unique picture in that it does not appear in any of the authoritative catalogues of mediaeval iconography, nor have we so far found any similar pictures in embroidery, manuscripts or other media. The High Priest, wearing a flat hat and sporting a beard, stands with the Palm of Paradise in his hand addressing his followers. In the words of a medieval mystery play, "Ye Jews that langour in this great infirmity, believeth in Christ Jesu and ye shall have health, through virtue of this holy palm that comes from the trinity, your sickness shall assuage and restore you to wealth".

So they were all converted and restored to health.

Fig 93. The Conversion and Healing of the Jews.

Fig 94.

'The apostles now took Mary's body and laid it in the tomb. Then as the Lord had commanded, they sat around the sepulcher.' [The Golden Legend Vol2.,p.81]

THE BURIAL OF THE VIRGIN

We now move to the left of the left-hand window still in the top tier. Mary's body is laid in a red sarcophagus by Saint John on the right and another figure to the left of him (now mostly disappeared). There were probably other figures in this scene - Buckler's sketch shows four definitely, with the extra two at the left hand end of the tomb.

The scene from the manuscript picture in Queen Mary's Psalter from the British Library (Fig.96) shows a similar number of people around Mary's body.

Fig 95. Mary's body is laid in the tomb.

Fig 96. The same scene from Queen Mary's Psalter, now in the British Library.

'Thomas was suddenly brought to the Mount of Olives and saw the holy body being taken up, and cried out to Mary: 'make thy servant glad by thy mercy, for now thou goest to heaven'. And the girdle with which the apostles had girt the body was thrown down to him; he took it and went to the valley of Josaphat.' [The Apocryphal New Testament, p.217]

Fig 97.

The careful arrangement of the pictures in narrative sequence is now slightly upset because of the artist's desire to have the crowning of Mary as Queen of Heaven on the East wall opposite the Christ's Ascension. So we turn now to the East wall and the centre and bottom pictures on the South side.

THE ASSUMPTION and

SAINT THOMAS RECEIVES THE GIRDLE

The apochryphal Joseph of Arimethea narrative tells how after the Apostles have laid Mary in the tomb, the angels come and raise her up and carry her up to heaven.

At this point St. Thomas, who was saying Mass in India, is suddenly transported to the Mount of Olives where he witnesses Mary's body being carried up to heaven by a host of angels. He cries out to Mary in joy and her girdle is dropped down to him. Our pictures show Thomas at the left hand side of the empty tomb, with the girdle in his hand, while above the empty tomb, the Virgin floats upwards with her hands at prayer, supported by two angels. Only one of them remains very visible on the left with head, shoulders and wings and one hand grasping Mary's elbow.

Visible across Thomas' head and stretching to the right is the second inscription described in more detail on page 76.

The accompanying picture from an Italian manuscript of the Life of the Virgin and of Christ dating to c.1400AD (Fig.100) shows the Virgin surrounded by a host of angels with the girdle in her hand, while Thomas kneels on the left. Whereas in the stained glass window at The Assumption of the Blessed Virgin Mary Church at Beckley, just north of Oxford, angels are seen carrying Mary up in what looks like a blanket (Fig.99).

Fig 98. The Assumption and Thomas receiving the Girdle, as it is today.

Fig 99. The scene in the East Window of the Church of the Assumption of the Blessed Virgin Mary at Beckley, Oxfordshire.

Fig 100. The scene in the Italian manuscript shows a whole squadron of angels carrying Mary !

Fig 101.

'When he (Thomas) had greeted the apostles, Peter said: "Thou wast always unbelieving, and so the Lord hath not suffered thee to be at his mother's burial"...Then he said: "Where have ye laid her body ?" and they pointed to the sepulchre. But he said: "The holy body is not there". Peter said: "Formerly you would not believe in the resurrection of the Lord before you touched him ; how should you believe us ?" Thomas went on saying : "It is not here". Then in anger they went and took away the stone, and the body was not there; and they knew not what to say, being vanquished by Thomas' words. Then Thomas told his story and showed them the girdle.' [The Apochryphal New Testament pp217,218]*

THE APOSTLES AT TABLE

This scene is in the centre of the wall below the Burial of the Virgin and shows five apostles gathered round a table with a sixth figure facing them at the left-hand (east) end.

So this picture depicts Thomas showing the girdle to the other apostles.

I have not yet found another representation of this exact scene. The scene from the Italian 15th century manuscript of the Life of the Virgin and of Christ shows Thomas giving the girdle to Peter while the rest of the disciples kneel round Mary's empty tomb (Fig.103). The tomb in this picture is represented as an open hole in the ground, whereas our tombs are shown as upright monuments.

Fig 102. Thomas shows the girdle to the Apostles.

Fig 103. Thomas shows Peter the girdle while the Apostles marvel at the empty tomb, from the 15th century Italian manuscript.

THE APOSTLES AT THE EMPTY TOMB (?)

The next picture in the sequence is then the one below the previous one, and now obliterated by the memorial to Katherine Villiers, the daughter of the Rev'd George Villiers, one-time Vicar of Chalgrove.

It is possible that this showed the apostles standing at the empty tomb having gone there in disbelief at Thomas' claim that Mary's body was not there. One account of the story states that the empty tomb was filled with flowers. All that we can see, however, is a small head to the top and left of the Villiers memorial.

Was this picture something like the one on the previous page (Fig.103) from the Italian manuscript where Thomas hands the girdle to Peter? and is it Thomas' head that we see? Or was it perhaps like the bottom half of the painting of the Assumption by Bartolomeo della Gatta (fig.106), which is now in the Diocesan Museum in Cortona, in which the apostles stand around the flower filled tomb?

Fig 104. The Villiers memorial.

Fig 105. The head top left of the Villiers memorial

Fig. 106 The Assumption and Thomas receiving the Girdle, by Bartolomeo della Gatta, 15thC, now in the Diocesan Museum in Cortona, Italy.

Fig 107.

'..on this day the celestial militia came to meet the mother of God with festive celebration and shone round about her with dazzling light, leading her up to the throne of God with lauds and spiritual canticles, and that the army of the heavenly Jerusalem exulted with indescribable joy, and welcomed her with ineffable devotion and boundless rejoicing....the Saviour himself went to meet his mother joyfully and gladly placed her on a throne at his side.' [The Golden Legend Vol 2 page 84]

THE CORONATION OF THE VIRGIN

The final picture in the sequence is above The Assumption and shows Mary on the left sitting on a bench next to and facing Jesus on the right who raises his hand over her head, either in blessing or, more likely, to place a crown upon her head. Above Mary's head, emerging from the side of the window splay, there is what remains of an angel swinging a censer which can just be seen about a foot below its head.

This is again a fairly popular and standard representation of this scene which can be seen in many manuscripts, as well as ivories such as the French 14th century ivory on display in the Victoria & Albert Museum, and again in the East Window at Beckley Church (Fig.109) just outside Oxford. There is also a good mosaic picture of this scene by Gaddo Gaddi on the west end wall of the Duomo in Florence dating from the 1340s.

Fig 108. Mary is crowned as Queen of Heaven. Mary and Jesus sit on a bench and Jesus on the right places the crown on Mary's head, while angels fly down from above

Fig 109. The Coronation as portrayed in the East Window at Beckley church, c 1325 -1350AD.

THE INSCRIPTIONS ON THE EAST WALL

There are two lines of text which run across the scenes of the Harrowing of Hell and Saint Thomas receiving the girdle. The lines formed in the plaster on which this text is written were placed in the plaster when it was still wet so it is fairly safe to believe that the inscriptions are contemporary with the paintings. They appear to be a prayer to Mary on behalf of the sponsors of the paintings.

The inscriptions are written in Latin and use abbreviated words. For example, for 'animabus' the word 'āibus' is written. The inscription over the Harrowing of Hell is believed to read "Orate....Jesu animabus dominorum Wabor". It is less decipherable over Saint Thomas but clearly begins with Maria and probably read something along the lines of "Sancta Maria, Dei genetrix, mater domini nostri Jesu Christi". So the whole prayer put together might read "Saint Mary, begetter of God, mother of our Lord Jesus Christ, pray to [our Saviour] Jesus for the souls of the Lords of Warborough", an appropriate prayer to Saint Mary, to whom this whole work and the church is dedicated, by the sponsors of the work, the de Barentyn family.

Fig 110 [above] The text over the Harrowing of Hell

Fig 111 [below] The text over Thomas receiving the Girdle

Fig 112.

THE LAST JUDGEMENT OR "DOOM"

In the south west corner of the chancel is a scene representing the Last Judgement. These "Dooms" are a very popular subject in mediaeval English churches and are often placed over the chancel arch facing the main body of the church as this arch symbolised the division between this world and the next. Such a Doom can be seen in the church of Saint James the Great at South Leigh just outside Witney in Oxfordshire (Fig.116).

Our Doom, however, is incorporated into the main scheme of paintings in the chancel, because of Mary's association with the Last Judgement as a mediator for mankind. The scene is placed in the south west corner so that it can be viewed through the squint window from the side chapel.

At the top of the scene Jesus, clearly showing the stigmata in his hands, side and feet, sits on a rainbow signifying the covenant made by God with mankind after the Flood. Next to him, Mary kneels in supplication baring her breast, the meaning of this icon being that as she tenderly served Jesus as a baby so now must Jesus be tender and loving to mankind. To the left of Mary, an angel with a horn (sadly no longer visible) flies down the side of the window arch sounding the last trump. Below them are two tiers of souls rising from their graves, including Bishops, monks, ladies and men, some with crosses on their shrouds. The centre figure in the upper tier with three chevrons on his hat is a Pope, while the centre figure in the lower tier is a secular priest, perhaps the man under whose direction the chancel was rebuilt and decorated. On the right between the two tiers of souls and Jesus above are what is left of another angel flying down the side of the wall.

Fig 113. The Doom - top tier. Jesus sits in judgement.

Fig 114. The Doom - middle tier. A Pope and others rise from their tombs, while an angel flies down the right hand side

Fig 115. The Doom - lower tier. More souls arise from their tombs.

Fig 116. The Doom in Saint James the Great Church at South Leigh in Oxfordshire. The centre scene over the chancel arch shows the angel playing the Last Trump, souls rising from their tombs and being weighed in the balance by St.Michael.

Fig.117 On the right hand wall, the damned are welcomed into the jaws of Hell.

Fig.118 On the left hand wall St.Peter with his key welcomes the righteous into heaven.

Fig 119.

SAINTS IN WINDOW ALCOVES

In all the chancel windows, except the window of The Annunciation, there are two saints, one on each side, and as in the main scheme of paintings they are drawn in such a way as to tell us who they are.

SAINT HELEN

In the north east window, on the left hand side is Saint Helen of the True Cross. Alas! all that is left of this painting now is the charming face of Saint Helen, although originally she stood complete with the Cross beside her, so that we should know who she is. Saint Helen is the patron saint of our sister church in this parish at Berrick Salome but her association with Mary is unclear. According to "The Golden Legend", Volume 1 Chapter 68, Saint Helen was sent to Jerusalem by her son, Emperor Constantine (the Younger) to find the True Cross some 270 years after the Crucifixion. With the aid of a Jewish wise man called Judas, Saint Helen found all three crosses and Jesus' cross was identified by the miracles it brought about. Today there are not many remaining images of Saint Helen and the two shown are an impression taken from a 13th century matrix (or seal) found in the Pilgrim's Hostel at Elstow (Fig.122) and a portion of stained glass window of the Norfolk School dating from the second half of the 15th century which can be seen in the V&A Museum (Fig.121).

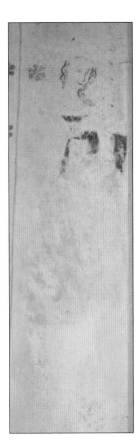

Fig 120. All that remains of Saint Helen of the True Cross today.

Fig.121 Saint Helen in a stained glass window of the Norwich School, second half of 15th century.

Fig 122. Impression taken from a 13th century matrix found in the Pilgrim's Hostel at Elstow, now in the British Library.

SAINT MARY MAGDALENE

Opposite Saint Helen is what remains of Saint Mary Magdalene, (fig 123), placed close to the Crucifixion scenes. Her right hand is held in a strange way and, although it has now disappeared, she probably held her emblem of the alabaster jar of spikenard oil with which she anointed Jesus' feet at the house in Bethany [John 12.3] Her left hand is held up apparently indicating the crucifixion scene on the adjacent wall. She can be seen with her jar emblem in many paintings and statues, for example in the painting (Fig.124) on the underside of the sarcophagus of the Duchess of Suffolk in St.Mary's Church, Ewelme, Oxfordshire, although you have to prostrate yourself to be able to see it ! She also has the jar tucked in her left arm in the painted miniature on the side of the golden head of the mediaeval Reichenau crozier, dated 1351AD, in the Victoria & Albert Museum (Figs.125 and 126).

But on the exquisitely carved wooden altar piece from Jonsberg in Sweden, (Fig.127) dating from the 1510's and now in the Historiska Museum in Stockholm, we find Mary Magdalene in a very similar pose to that depicted in our wall painting (only in mirror image). The scene of the Descent from the Cross, on the Jonsberg altar piece (fig.128) shows Mary Magdalene in close proximity, as she is in our paintings.

Fig.127 Mary Magdalene in the Jonsberg Altarpiece

Fig.123 Mary Magdalene

Fig 124 A copy of the painting of Mary Magdalene on the underside of the tomb of the Duchess of Suffolk in St. Mary's church, Ewelme.

Fig.125 The Reichenau Crozier.

Fig. 126 A close up of Mary Magdalene on the Reichenau Crozier

Fig. 128 The Descent from the Cross on the Jonsberg altar piece with Mary Magdalene in close attendance

Fig 129. Saint Peter and Saint Paul

'So (Nero) the emperor gave Peter and Paul into the hands of Paulinus … Then Peter, being an alien, was condemned to be crucified, while Paul, because he was a Roman citizen, was sentenced to beheading.' [The Golden Legend, Vol 1 pp344, 345]

SAINT PETER

To the left of the east window is a large representation of Saint Peter, who holds in his left hand the keys to the Kingdom of Heaven and in his right hand a book (which is no longer visible). In "The Golden Legend" we are told that 'when Peter came to the cross he said "Because my Lord came down from heaven to earth, his cross was raised straight up; but he deigns to call me from earth to heaven, and my cross should have my head toward the earth and should point my feet toward heaven. Therefore, since I am not worthy to be on the cross the way my Lord was, turn my cross and crucify me head down!" So they turned the cross and nailed him to it with his feet upwards and his hands downwards.'

SAINT PAUL

Opposite him on the right hand side of the east window is Saint Paul, with his emblem, a sword, nonchalantly resting on his shoulder. Paul was martyred by being beheaded with a sword, a right he claimed as a Roman citizen.

Both Peter and Paul are clearly visible with their emblems on the Syon cope in the Victoria & Albert Museum (Page 92, and Fig.132 and 133). Paul can also be seen top left on the Brass memorial from the French Bishop's tomb on page 87 .

Fig 130. Saint Peter on the left hand side of the East Window

Fig 131. Saint Paul on the right hand side of the East Window.

Fig 132. Saint Peter on the Syon Cope.

Fig 133. Saint Paul on the Syon Cope.

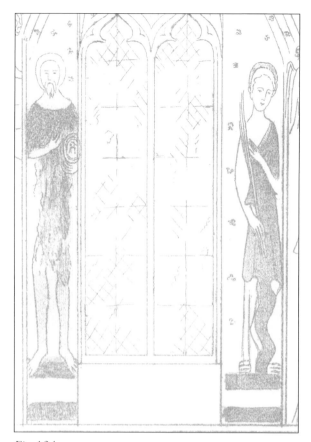

Fig 134.

'In those days John the Baptist appeared in the wilderness of Judea....Now John wore clothing of camel's hair with a leather belt around his waist, and his food was locusts and wild honey.' [Matthew 3 vv 1-4]

'The revelation of Jesus Christ, which God gave him to show his servants what must soon take place; he made it known by sending his angel to his servant John, who testified to the word of God and to the testimony of Jesus Christ, even to all that he saw.' [The Revelation 1 vv1-2]

SAINT JOHN THE BAPTIST

Moving to the south east window, we find on the left hand side a man dressed in clothes of camel's hair and cradling in his left arm a halo ring containing a small lamb, the Agnus Dei, the Lamb of God. This is, of course, John the Baptist. Another ivory, the left side of a diptych, in the British Museum shows John in this posture (Fig.138).

SAINT JOHN THE EVANGELIST

Opposite him stands a young man holding the palm of paradise, which the Virgin Mary had given him. This is Saint John the Evangelist, placed close to the story of the death and assumption of Mary, in which he played an important part as we have read above. A brass memorial to an unknown 14th century Flemish Bishop, also in the British Museum, has a similar picture of John (Fig.136).

Fig 135. Saint John the Evangelist with the Palm of Paradise.

Fig 136. The brass from an unknown French Bishop's tomb showing Saint John the Evangelist (top left) with the Palm of Paradise

Fig 137. Saint John the Baptist in the wallpaintings

Fig 138. Saint John the Baptist in an ivory carved diptych in the British Museum

Fig 139. Saint Laurence left and Saint Bartholomew right in the South West window of the Chancel.

'(The Emperor) Decius said to Laurence:"Either you will sacrifice to the gods, or you will spend the night being tortured." Laurence: "My night has no darkness, and all things gleam in the light!" Decius gave his orders: "Let an iron bed be brought, and let this stubborn Laurence rest on it!". The executioners therefore stripped him, laid him out on the iron grill, piled burning coals under it, and pressed heated iron pitchforks upon his body.' [The Golden Legend, Vol II p 66]

'When Bartholomew was brought before him, the king said "So you are the one who subverted my brother!" The

apostle: 'I did not subvert him, I converted him!" ... Hearing this, the king tore the purple robe he was wearing, and ordered the apostle to be beaten with clubs and flayed alive.' [The Golden Legend, Vol II p112]

SAINT LAURENCE

Finally, in the south west window, on the left is Saint Laurence who was a Roman Deacon, hence the book which he holds in his right hand. He was martyred a few days after Pope Sixtus II in the persecution of the Emperor Valerian in 258AD. Legend has it that he was roasted alive on a gridiron, and with his left hand he points down to the gridiron standing in front of him. Another picture of Saint Laurence comes from Saint Cuthbert's stole, 934AD, which can be seen in the museum at Durham Cathedral (Fig.142).

SAINT BARTHOLEMEW

Opposite Saint Laurence stands Saint Bartholomew who holds in his hand a large flaying knife, by which, according to the Roman Martyrology, he was skinned alive before being beheaded at his martyrdom in Armenia. Saint Bartholomew is also to be seen on the Syon Cope in the Victoria & Albert Museum and in the wooden retable from Ganthem Church, Sweden, c 1350AD, which can be seen in the Historiska Museum in Stockholm (Fig.143).

Fig 140. Saint Laurence with his book and gridiron.

Fig 141. Saint Bartholomew with his flaying knife.

Fig 142. Saint Laurence on the embroidered stole of Saint Cuthbert in Durham Cathedral Museum.

Fig 143. Saint Bartholomew on the wooden retable from Ganthem Church, Sweden.

THE QUATREMAINE MEMORIAL

At the west end of the Nave on the wall adjacent to the bell tower is a painted memorial to members of the Quatremaine family dating from 1692. Such painted memorials are rare in England. This memorial used to be on the east wall of the Saint James' Chapel on the north side of the window but was carefully removed for cleaning and restoration by the late Eve Baker in 1984 and was then placed in its present position.

OTHER WALL PAINTINGS

When it was removed from the Saint James' Chapel, some earlier paintings were revealed underneath, Fig 145, which were themselves cleaned and restored in 1993 and can now be clearly seen. Eve Baker wrote of this painting "It is certainly much earlier than any of the other paintings. As far as I could see, it continued on the north aisle wall and on the south side area; but I did not uncover more." This painting looks like a decorated tower with pinnacles on either side and a banner flying from the centre pinnacle. Such towers and pinnacles can be seen in other medieval pictures, Fig 146. Lower down there are the remains of an inscription which has yet to be deciphered, Fig 147.

As Clive Rouse points out in his book 'Medieval Wall Paintings' "… all medieval churches in England were more or less completely painted" . In fact these paintings have now been dated to the middle or latter part of the 14th century so would probably have followed on from the completion of the work in the chancel.

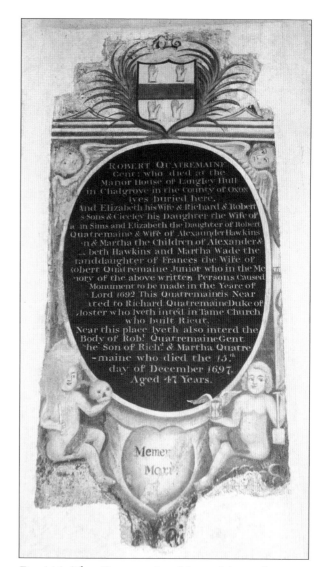

Fig 144. The Quatremaine Memorial on the west wall of the Nave.

Fig 145. The original wall paintings on the east wall of the Saint James' Chapel.

Fig 146. Tower and flags in the 14th century wall painting in St James the Great Church at South Leigh, Oxfordshire

Fig 147. A close up of the lower part of the painting showing the inscription.

Fig.148 The Syon Cope now in the V&A Museum, London

Fig. 149 The carved ivory Diptych by the Master of
Kremsmunster, now in the Staatliche Museum in
Berlin

18

127,
128,
143

15, 45,
38, 121,
etc.

125, 149

136

22, 32, 42,
61, 65

81, 84,
100, 103,
106

Fig. 150 Countries of origin of some of the items illustrated in this guide. The numbers relate to figure numbers.

REFERENCES AND FURTHER READING

A Collection of Articles, Injunctions, Canons, Orders, Ordinances, and Constitutions Ecclesiastical; With other Publick Records of the Church of England. Printed for Robert Pawlet, at the Bible in Chancery Lane, near Fleetstreet, 1675.

A Study of the wall paintings in the chancel of St.Mary's, Chalgrove, A Dissertation submitted towards the Degree of Master of Arts in Medieval Studies. S.T.J.Maynard, Centre for Medieval Studies, University of York, 1986.

On Mural Paintings in Chalgrove Church,Oxfordshire. Communicated through J.H.Parker, Esq. F.S.A. William Burges, Esq. Archaeologia Volume xxxviii, pp431-8, 1860.

The Golden Legend, Readings on the Saints. Jacobus de Voragine, translated by W G Ryan, Princeton University Press, 1993

The Apocryphal New Testament. Translated by M.R.James, Oxford University Press, Reprinted 1989.

A Survey of Manuscripts illuminated in the British Isles. Volume Five. Gothic Manuscripts [I] 1285 - 1385, Professor Lucy Freeman Sandler, General Editor J.J.G.Alexander, Harvey Miller Publishers, Oxford University Press, 1986.

English Wall-paintings of the Fourteenth Century. E.W.Tristram, Routledge & Paul, London, 1955.

Medieval Wall Paintings. E.Clive Rouse, Shire Publications Ltd, 1991.

Medieval Craftsmen - Painters. Paul Binski, British Museum Press, 1991

The Stripping of the Altars. Eamon Duffy, Yale University Press, 1992

Thomas Cranmer. Diarmaid MacCulloch, Yale University Press, 1996

ACKNOWLEDGEMENTS

Quotations from the following publications are used by kind permission of the copyright holders:

New Revised Standard Version Bible, Copyright © 1989, Division of Christian Education of the National Council of the Churches of Christ in the United States of America. Used by permission. All rights reserved.

Jacobus de Voragine; The Golden Legend. Copyright ©1993 by PUP. Reprinted by permission of Princeton University Press.

Montague Rhodes Jones; The Apocryphal New Testament. Copyright © 1924 by OUP. Reprinted by permission of Oxford University Press.

PHOTOGRAPHIC CREDITS

Photographs: M Beulah, fig 8; V&A Picture Library, fig 15 (8128-1863), fig 26 (28G-1892), figs 32 and 75 (211-1865), fig 45 (T.31-1936), fig 126 (7950-1862), fig 148 (82-1864); © Copyright British Museum, fig 12 (1925, 0507.1), figs 22 and 65 (Dalton 284), fig 23 (1983, 7-4.1), fig 136 (1853,0221.1), fig 138 (Dalton 246); Aal Church, Norway, fig 18; John Steel-Clark, figs 21, 28, 83, 87, 120, 130, 131, 135 & 137; The Bodleian Library, University of Oxford, fig 29 (MS. Laud Misc. 188, fol. 41r), fig 38 (MS. Gough liturg. D. 8, fol. 37v), fig 46 (MS. Gough liturg. D. 8, fol. 49r), fig 49 (MS. Gough liturg. D. 8, fol. 49v), fig 55 (MS. Gough liturg. D. 8, fol. 61v), fig 58 (MS. Gough liturg. D. 8, fol. 62r), fig 62 (MS. Gough liturg. D. 8, fol. 62v), fig 68 (MS. Gough liturg. D. 8, fol. 71), fig 84 (MS, Canon.Ital. 275, fol. 50r), fig 100 (MS, Canon.Ital. 280, fol. 242r), fig 103 (MS, Canon.Ital. 280, fol. 242v); By permission of the Master and Fellows of St.John's College, Cambridge, fig 35 (MS. K.21, fol. 49v); Fitzwilliam Museum, Cambridge, fig 42 (M.9-1938); By permission of the Master and Fellows of Trinity College, Cambridge, fig 52 (MS O.4.16 f.113v); Alain Renaud, fig 61; By kind permission of Staatliche Museen Zu Berlin Preussischer Kulturbesitz, figs 72, 78, 85 & 149 (Inv.Nr. 2722); © Photo SCALA, Florence, fig 81 (code 84736); By permission of The British Library, figs 88 & 96 (Royal 2B VII f298a), fig 122 (Seals CLXXX2); Nicholas Meyjes, figs 99 & 109; By kind permission of Museo Diocesano Cortona, fig 106; Lennart Karlsson, Bild Data Projektet, fig 127 (Jonsberg 93:327:07), fig 128 (Jonsberg 93:326:31); By kind permission of the Chapter of Durham Cathedral, fig 142; Statens Historiska Museer, Stockholm, fig 143 (Inv.Nr.11365); all other photographs by the author. The drawings by C.A.Buckler are taken from Archaeologia, published by the Society of Antiquaries of London, Volume XXXVIII, MDCCCLX, plates XXIII and XXIV p.436.